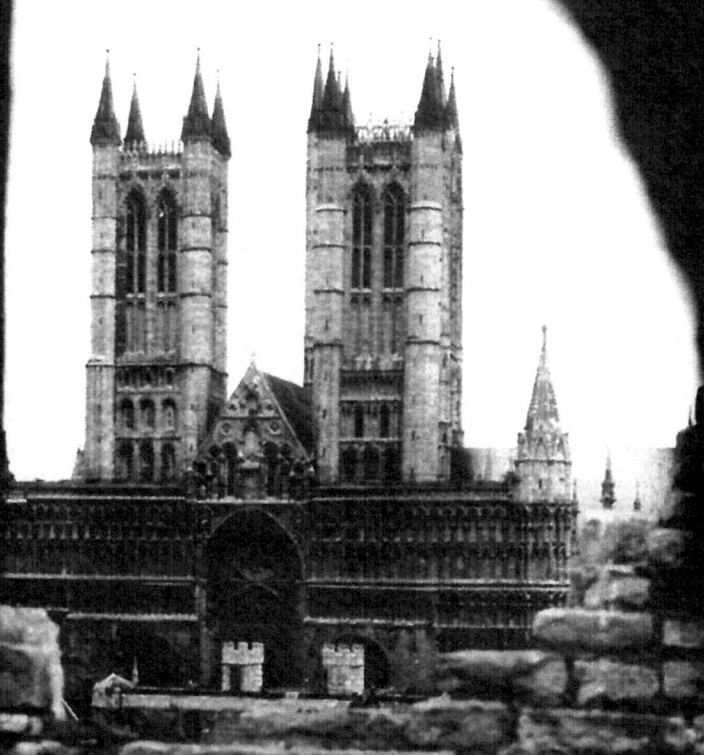

Enjoy the pilgrimage,
Bon Camimo
Revd. John N. Merrill

Greetings Pilgrim.

May you rest a while and find the Peace of the Lord in this place.

Christ has no body now but yours.
No hands, no feet on earth, but yours.
Yours are the eyes
through which Christ
looks compassion into the world.
Yours are the feet with
which Christ walks to do good.
Yours are the hands
with which Christ
blesses the world.

St. Teresa of Avila.

WHY I WALK by Revd. John N. Merrill

I walk for the exercise; to stretch my legs and muscles; to suck in the fresh air and be free in the wide, wide world, as I walk upon Mother Earth.

I walk to see the trees; that sway in the breeze. To watch the leaves flutter in summer and to walk through on the ground in November. I observe the quietness of winter and watch the buds form ready to emerge when it is their time.

I walk to see the wild flowers; the wood anemones, the blue bells, red campion, and orchids that grow in Spring and early summer.

I walk to listen to the birds that sing in the hedgerows and trees. The friendly Robin is not far away, the started Jay or motionless heron standing at the waters edge. A sudden flash of blue as a kingfisher shoots by.

I walk to see the wild animals; the red fox, the deer, the squirrel and the insects and butterflies, like the dragonfly and red admiral butterfly.

I walk to see the views; to ascend a lofty peak and sit upon the summit surveying everything below, like an eagle high in the air.

I walk for solitude; peace and quiet, to go back to the basics of life, where it is just man and the elements.

I walk in the sunshine, the rain, snow and wind. All has its own beauty and characteristic. All are the cycles of life. I admire the cloudless sky and the rolling clouds of wind and storm.

I walk to see the work of man and God, knowing that we are all connected. Everything has its own beauty.

As the sun sets and I walk home, I know I have lived and experienced a full day, witnessing the whole spectrum of life. I am grateful, very grateful, that God gave me two fine legs, a healthy heart and good lungs to see paradise on Earth.

© Revd. John N. Merrill 2012

HOW TO DO A WALK

The walks in this book follow public right of ways, be it a footpath, bridleway, Boat or Rupp. which are marked on the Ordnance Survey 1:25,000 Explorer Series of maps.

On each walk I have detailed which map are needed and I would urge you to carry and use a map. As I walk I always have the map out on the section I am walking, constantly checking that I am walking the right way. Also when coming to any road or path junction, I can check on the map to ensure I take the right route.

Most paths are signed and waymarked with coloured arrows - yellow for footpaths; blue for bridleways - but I would at best describe them as intermittent. They act as confirmation of the right of way you are walking and the arrow usually point in the direction of travel.

The countryside has the added problem of vandalism and you will find path logo's and Information Boards spray painted over and even path signs pointing the wrong way! That is why I always advise carrying the map open on the area you are walking to check you are walking the right way. In my walking instructions I have given the name and number of each main and minor road, canal lock and bridge number, together with house numbers where you turn and the name of the inns passed. Wherever I add what the footpath sign says, plus the stiles, footbridges and kissing gates en route. All to help you have a smooth and trouble free walk.

I confirm that I have walked every route and written what I found at the time of walking.

Most people don't walk correctly with a straight spine and feet parallel to each other, and a few inches apart. Each step starts the cycle of lifting the foot a little way off the ground and placing the heel down first, then moving forward as the foot bends with the toes being last to leave the ground as the cycle begins again. It is all a gentle fluid rolling motion; with practice you can glide across the terrain, effortlessly, for mile after mile.

A walker.

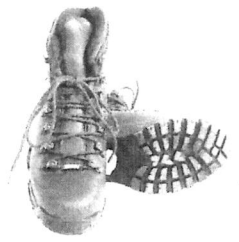

There is a walker who in his youth walked up hill and down dale. As the years passed he went for longer walks, not 20 or 30 miles or even 100 miles, but walks of a minimum of 1,000 miles. He progressed to 1,500 miles, then 2,100 miles and knew he was ready for the big one. 7,000 miles around Britain. He then left these shores and did long walks in Europe, America and Asia. So far has done more than 219,500 miles and written 450 books, while wearing out 134 pairs of boots. He has never been ill, or broken a bone or been in hospital. He has had no new knees or hips, he is in the same body that he was born with. Who is this man? Why me, Revd. John Merrill! *(Copyright - JNM October 31st. 2017)*

The John Merrill Foundation

- is a not for profit charitable Foundation, solely committed to ensuring the copyright, moral rights and writings of Revd. John Merrill are available to all.

The book was originally published by John Merrill and went through numerous reprintings. This Print-on-Demand edition was first printed in 2017.

All rights reserved.

I hope you enjoy
this walk to
St. Albans Shrine,
and may I wish you a
good Pilgrimage and
Happy Walking!
John N. Merrill

The Passionate Man's Pilgrimage
by Sir Walter Raleigh (1552? - 1618).

Give me my scallop shell of quiet,
My staff of faith to walk upon,
My scrip of joy, immortal diet,
My bottle of salvation,
My gown of glory, hope's true gage,
And thus I'll take my pilgrimage.

Blood must be my body's balmer;
No other balm will there be given;
Whilst my soul like quiet palmer,
Traveleth towards the land of heaven;
Over the silver mountains
Where spring the nectar fountains;
There will I kiss
The bowl of bliss;
And drink mine everlasting fill
Upon every milken hill.
My soul will be a-dry before;
But after it will thirst no more.

St. Albans Way

Waltham Abbey to St. Albans..

by Revd. John N. Merrill

Maps, sketches and photographs by John N. Merrill

"I hike the paths and trails of the world for others to enjoy."

The John Merrill Ministry

"The miracle of life is not to fly in the air, or walk on the water, but to walk upon the earth." CHINESE SAYING.

The Pilgrim Way Series Vol 8.

2012

Oak - from Epping Forest - carved monument in the grounds of Waltham Abbey.
Ancestor by Helena Stylianides with assistance from Brian Pattenden. 1992.

**THE JOHN MERRILL FOUNDATION,
32, Holmesdale, Waltham Cross,
Hertfordshire. EN8 8QY**

Tel. 01992 - 762776
Email - marathonhiker@aol.com
www.johnmerrillwalkguides.co.uk
www.thejohnmerrillministry.co.uk

International Copyright - Revd. John N. Merrill.
All rights reserved. No part of this publication may be reproduced or transmitted in any form or by any means electronic or mechanical including photocopy, recording or information storage or retrieval system in any place, in any country without the prior permission of The John Merrill Foundation.

Revd. John N. Merrill asserts his moral rights to be identified as the author and illustrator of this work.

A catalogue record for this book is available from the British Library.

Conceived, edited, typset and designed by Revd. John N. Merrill.
Printed and handmade by Revd. John N. Merrill.
Book layout and cover design by Revd. John N. Merrill.

Copyright - Text, maps and photographs - Revd. John N. Merrill 2017

ISBN 978-0-9553691-3-1

First published - August 2006. Reprinted and revised - November 2017 - Special limited edition. Cover picture - by Revd. John N. Merrill.

Please note - The maps in this guide are purley illustrative to gikve uolu an obverall picture of the route. You are encouraged to the use the appropriate O.S. 1:25,000 Explorer Sereies maps as detailed in the book.

Typset in Avenir Next Demi - bold, italic and plain - 10pt, 14pt and 18pt.

John Merrill confirms that he has walked all the routes in this book and detailed what he found at the time of walking. The publishers, however cannot be held responsible for alterations, errors, omissions, or for changes in details given. They welcome information to help keep the book upto date.

The John Merrill Foundation maintains the John Merrill Library and archives and administers the worldwide publishing rights of John Merrill's works in all media formats.

The John Merrill Foundation plants sufficient trees through the Woodland Trust to replenish the trees used in its publications.

John at the end of his walk to Chartres Cathedral, from Notre Dame, Paris - August 2017.

A little about Revd. John N. Merrill

John is unique, possessing the skills of a marathon runner, mountain climber and athlete. Since his first 1,000 mile walk through the islands of the Inner and Outer Hebrides in 1970, he has since walked over 219,000 miles and worn out 134 pairs of boots, 49 rucksacks and more than 1,600 pairs of socks. He has brought marathon walking to Olympic standard. In 1978 he became the first person to walk around the entire coastline of Britain - 7,000 miles. He has walked across Europe, the Alps and Pyrenees - 3,000 miles with 600,000 feet of ascent and descent. In America he has walked the 2,500 mile Appalachian Trail; the Pacific Crest Trail - 2,500 miles in record time; the Continental Divide Trail; became the first person to thru-hike the Buckeye Trail - 1,350 miles in Ohio and completed a unique 4,260 mile walk in 178 days coast to coast across America. He has climbed all the mountains in New Mexico and walked all the trails.

In Britain he has walked all the National Trails many times - The Cleveland Way 13 times! and the Pennine Way four times in 4 months. He has linked all the National Parks and trails in a 2,060 mile walk; completed a 1,608 mile Land's End to John o' Groats walk and countless other unique walks. He has walked three times to Santiago de Compostella via different routes; to St. Olav's Shrine in Norway - 420 miles; walked to Assisi, St. Gilles du Gard, the Cathar Ways and to Mont St. Michel, twice. He has walked every long distance path in France and Germany, and walked to every pilgrimage destination in England and France, and extensively walked in every country in Europe. His latest pilgrimage was from Caen to Mont St. Michel in September 2017.

He has walked in Africa; all the trails in the Hong Kong Islands; and completed five trekking expeditions to the Himalayas and India. Not only is he the world's leading marathon walker he is Britain's most experienced walker. John is author of more than 450 walk guides which have sold more than 4 million copies with more than 1 million sold on the Peak District alone. He has created more than 80 challenge walks which have been used to raise, so far, more than a £1 million for different charities.

John has never broken a bone or been lost and never had any trouble anywhere. He still walks in the same body he was born with, has had no replacements and does not use poles. This he puts down to his deep spiritual nature and in 2010 he was ordained as a multi-faith Minister - a universal monk, "honouring and embracing all faiths and none". *He conducts weddings and funerals services all over UK and abroad. He teaches Qigong and is a Reiki practioner. He gives illustrated talks on his walks all over the U.K.*

CONTENTS

Page No.

Introduction 7

How to do it 9

About the walk - some general comments..................................10

Equipment Notes - some personal thoughts...............................11

About Waltham Abbey - a few notes 12

Stage One - Waltham Abbey to Bury Green - 4 miles 14

Stage Two - Bury Green to Northaw - 5 miles 20

Stage Three - Northaw to North Mymms - 6 miles 24

Stage Four - North Mymms to Tyttenhanger - 4 1/2 miles 30

Stage Five - Tyttenhanger to St. Albans Cathedral - 4 1/2 miles 34

A little about the Cathedral and Abbey Church of St. Albans 38

Walk Record Log 41

Pilgrim Certificate Order Form 42

Why I go on a Pilgrimage 43

The Pilgrims Way Series 45

Other Books by John N. Merrill 46

Lectures and Talks by John N. Merrill 48

The Shrine of Saint Alban; St. Albans Cathedral.

INTRODUCTION

For a long while I wanted to link these two Abbey Churches and pilgrimage centres together, as a pilgrimage walk. First it was to be a Spring walk when the daffodils were in full bloom, but somehow the time slipped by. Finally, one very hot mid summer day, I set off at 8.0. a.m. and walked from the west door of Waltham Abbey Church to the west door of St. Albans Cathedral and Abbey Church. There after some 26 miles of walking in 90° F heat, I couldn't find a bed and breakfast and caught the train back to Waltham Cross, where I had begun.

A week later I was back in St. Albans to look around the town and cathedral. As luck would have it I was here on St. James Day - patron saint of Spain and I have walked three times to his shrine in north-west Spain at Santiago de Compostela. Entering the cathedral just before noon I was told there was a Eucharist Service around St. Albans tomb, about to start. Perfect; and again I had been guided to here.

Waltham Cross's Eleanor Cross.

Both Waltham Abbey and St. Albans Cathedral are fascinating religious houses, based on Benedictine (St. Albans) and Augustinian (Waltham Abbey), and well worth a wander around. I always felt that monks would have travelled between the two abbeys centuries ago. But, it was not until I wandered around St. Albans did I learn there was another connection between these two places. On December 12th. 1290, the cortege of Queen Eleanor on its journey from Harby in Nottinghamshire, stopped over night in St. Albans. Each place where they stayed overnight an Eleanor Cross was built. The following day, 13th. December 1290, the cortege proceeded 25 miles to Waltham Abbey and a cross was built at the cross roads at the now present day Waltham Cross. The cross here is only one of three that survive today, built between 1291-1294 and restored in 1989. On December 14th. 1290 the cortege returned to the cross roads and proceeded southwards to the present day, Charing Cross.

There is also a more sinister link between the two places following a murder in Waltham Cross in 1914. A man slitting the throat of a woman, near the Four Swans Inn; the overhead inn sign still remains near the cross. The murderer was hung at St. Albans on December 23rd. 1914 and his body was left hanging for an hour! This was the last hanging in Hertfordshire.

My pilgrimage walk was very pleasant, despite the heat, first to the River LeeNavigation and then onto the New River. Next were tree lined paths and tracks which led me to the attractive Northaw village, with a church and green. I pressed on along paths to the historic North Mymms and its impressive hall and unspoilt 14th. century church. Then onto Colney Heath and the final paths around St. Albans to the cathedral. Like all walks the end was acknowledged and another pilgrimage was completed - thankfully my list of walks to do, gets bigger and bigger!

Here is a pilgrimage walk through Hertfordshire to a major medieval shrine and our largest cathedral. Although a long day's walk, it is relatively flat walking and well worth it and a service the following day completes the experience.

Have a good pilgrimage. and walk.   *Happy walking!*
John Merrill

Waltham Abbey Church.

HOW TO DO IT

The whole walk is covered by Ordnance Survey 1:25,000 Explorer Series Nos. -
- 174 - Epping Forest and Lee Valley.
- 182 - St. Albans & Hatfield.

The walk is planned to be done in a day - about 8 to 9 hours excluding stops. There are only limited facilities along the way - Inns at Northaw and Colney Heath. Shops at Colney Heath. There is no accommodation on the route and the nearest around the half way mark is at South Mimms, two miles south of the route. Potters Bar Station is 1/2 mile from route, little less than half way. Both Waltham Abbey and St. Albans have all facilities and full details can be had from their respective Tourist Information Centres. If you wish to do it stages the rail stations of Cuffley and Brookmans Park (for North Mymms) are within a mile of the route.

The route keeps to paths and tracks as much as possible, and road walking is kept to a minimum. The only long stretch is through Colney Heath - there is no alternative here, except making the walk an extra 5 miles long! Much of the route is level and only a handful of undulations along its entire length.

Basically carry what you need for the day and if you have a backup party, then both Northaw and Colney Heath would be good meet up points.

START AND END -

Waltham Cross is on the main line from London - Liverpool Street - and a short bus ride or walk will bring you to Waltham Abbey.

St. Albans has two train stations - The main one is on the direct line to Kings Cross, London. The Abbey Station goes to King's Cross via Watford.

WALTHAM ABBEY TOURIST OFFICE,
2, Highbridge Street,
Waltham Abbey,
Essex. EN9 1DG
Tel. 01992-652295

ST. ALBANS TOURIST OFFICE,
The Town Hall,
Market Place,
St. Albans,
Hertfordshire
AL3 5DJ
Tel. 01727-864511

ABOUT THE WALK

Whilst every care is taken detailing and describing the walks ikn this book, it should be borne in mind that the countryside changes witgh the seasons and the work of man. I have described the walks to the best of my ability, detailing what I have found actually on the walk in the way of stiles, kissing gates and signs. You should always walk with the appropriate O.S. map as detailed for each walk; open on the walk area for constant reference, or downladed onto your mobile phone. Obviously with the passage of time stiles become broken or replaced by kissing gates; inns change their name or have close down. Signs have a habit of being broken or pushed over and often they are pointing in the wrong direction! All the routes follow public rights of way and only rarely will you find a tree blown down across the path or an electric fence, requiring a small detour. Some rights of way are rerouted such as around a farm but they are generally well signed.

All rights of way have colour coded arrows on marker posts, stiles, gates, path posts, trees and these help you showing the direction of travel.

> YELLOW - Public footpath.
> BLUE - Public bridleway.
> RED - Byway open to all traffic (BOAT).
> BLACK - Road used as a public path (RUPP).
> WHITE - Concessionary and Permissive path.

The seasons bring occasional problems whilst out walking which should also be borne in mind. In the height of summer the paths become overgrown and you may have to fight your way through in a few places. In low lying areas the fields are full of crops. Usually a defined path leads through. In summer the ground is usually dry but in autumn and winter can be wet and slippery.

The mileage for each walk is based on several calculations -
1. My pedometer reading and steps taken - usually 2,000 to a mile.
2. The route on the map measured.
3. The time I took for the walk - the average person walks at 3mph - 2.5mph uphill.

Allow 20 mins for a mile; 10 mins for 1/2 mile and 5 mins for 1/4 mile.

"For every mile that you walk you extend your life by 21 mins."

EQUIPMENT NOTES

Today there is a bewildering variety of walking gear, much is superfluous to general walking in Britain. As a basic observation, people over dress for the outdoors. Basically equipment should be serviceable and do the task. I don't use walking poles; humans were built to walk with two legs! The following are some of my thoughts gathered from my walking experiences.

BOOTS - For summer use and day walking I wear lightweight boots. For high mountains and longer trips I prefer a good quality boot with a full leather upper, of medium weight, traditional style ,with a vibram sole. I always add a foam cushioned insole to help cushion the base of my feet.

SOCKS - I generally wear two thick pairs as this helps minimise blisters. The inner pair are of loop stitch variety and approximately 80% wool. The outer are also a thick pair of approximately 80% wool. I often wear double inner socks, which minimise blisters.

CLOTHES & WATERPROOFS - for general walking I wear a T shirt or cotton shirt with a cotton wind jacket on top, and shorts - even in snow! You generate heat as you walk and I prefer to layer my clothes to avoid getting too hot. Depending on the season will dictate how many layers you wear. In soft rain I just use my wind jacket for I know it quickly dries out. In heavy or consistent rain I slip on a poncho, which covers me and my pack and allows air to circulate, while keeping me dry. Only in extreme conditions will I don over-trousers, much preferring to get wet and feel comfortable. I never wear gaiters, except when cross country skiing, or in snow and glacier crossings. I find running shorts and sleeveless T shirts ideal for summer.

FOOD - as I walk I carry bars of chocolate, for they provide instant energy and are light to carry. In winter a flask of hot coffee is welcome. I never carry water and find no hardship from not doing so, but this is a personal matter! From experience I find the more I drink the more I want and sweat. You should always carry some extra food such as trail mix & candy bars etc., for emergencies. Full milk is a very underestimated source of food and liquid.

RUCKSACKS - for day walking I use a rucksack of about 30/40 litre capacity and although it leaves excess space it does mean that the sac is well padded, with an internal frame and padded shoulder straps, chest strap and waist strap. Inside apart from the basics for one day, in winter I carry gloves, wear a hat/cap and carry a spare pullover and a pair of socks.

MAP & COMPASS - when I am walking I always have the relevant map - preferably 1:25,000 scale - open in my hand. This enables me to constantly check that I am walking the right way. In case of bad weather I carry a compass, which once mastered gives you complete confidence in thick cloud or mist - you should always know where you are; I have a built in direction finder! Map reading and compass work is a skill and should be learnt. With modern technology you can now downloaded OS maps to your phone, record your walk, mileage, calories, steps taken, walking speed and time taken.

A LITTLE ABOUT WALTHAM ABBEY -

King Harold's Statue on the front righthand side

WALTHAM ABBEY CHURCH - Dedicated to the Holy Cross. This fine building was once one of England's largest monasteries. Outside the walls can be seen the resting place of King Harold, killed at the Battle of Hastings in 1066, with an arrow through his eye. He built the shrine, the second on this site, in 1060, with 13 secular canons. Here was kept the Holy Cross from Somerset, which he prayed before, resulting in his paralysis being healed. This led to the church being a major centre for pilgrimages, as more miracles occurred. The most notable feature inside are remarkable circular Norman pillars.

King Harold's resting place, outside the present building.

Rose and Lancet windows from the outside with King Harold's tomb site in the foreground.

14th. century Abbey Gatehouse with transport and pedestrian entrance archways.

In 1177, Henry II enlarged the church, as part of his penance for the murder of Thomas a Becket in Canterbury Cathedral in 1170. The building by this time was three times the present size. 26 Augustinian Cannons were installed and in 1184 it became an Abbey. Over the years it was one of the most prosperous and in 1540 was the last abbey to dissolved by Henry VIII. By good luck the canons church was separated by a low screen and the people of Waltham Abbey were able to claim this part as their parish church and it was saved. Outside you can see the extent of the monastery and cloisters, considerable walls, cloister gateway and 14th. century gatehouse with pedestrian and wheeled transport archways.

Inside are many interesting features; the Norman pillars and one on the south aisle can be seen the scratch marks made from the hanging chained bible. The purbeck marble font dates from the 12th. century. The tower has fourteen bells and is the only one constructed during Mary Tudor reign in 1556. In the north aisle is the only 13th. century memorial to an abbot.

The south aisle has a monument (1600) to the Denny family who took over the Abbey's land, after the dissolution. The nave ceiling is Victorian and the painted panels show the signs of the zodiac. The rose window and three lancet windows date from the 1860's.

There is much more to see and explore as you wander round, including the 14th. century Crypt and Lady Chapel.

Stage One -
WALTHAM ABBEY TO BURY GREEN
- 4 MILES

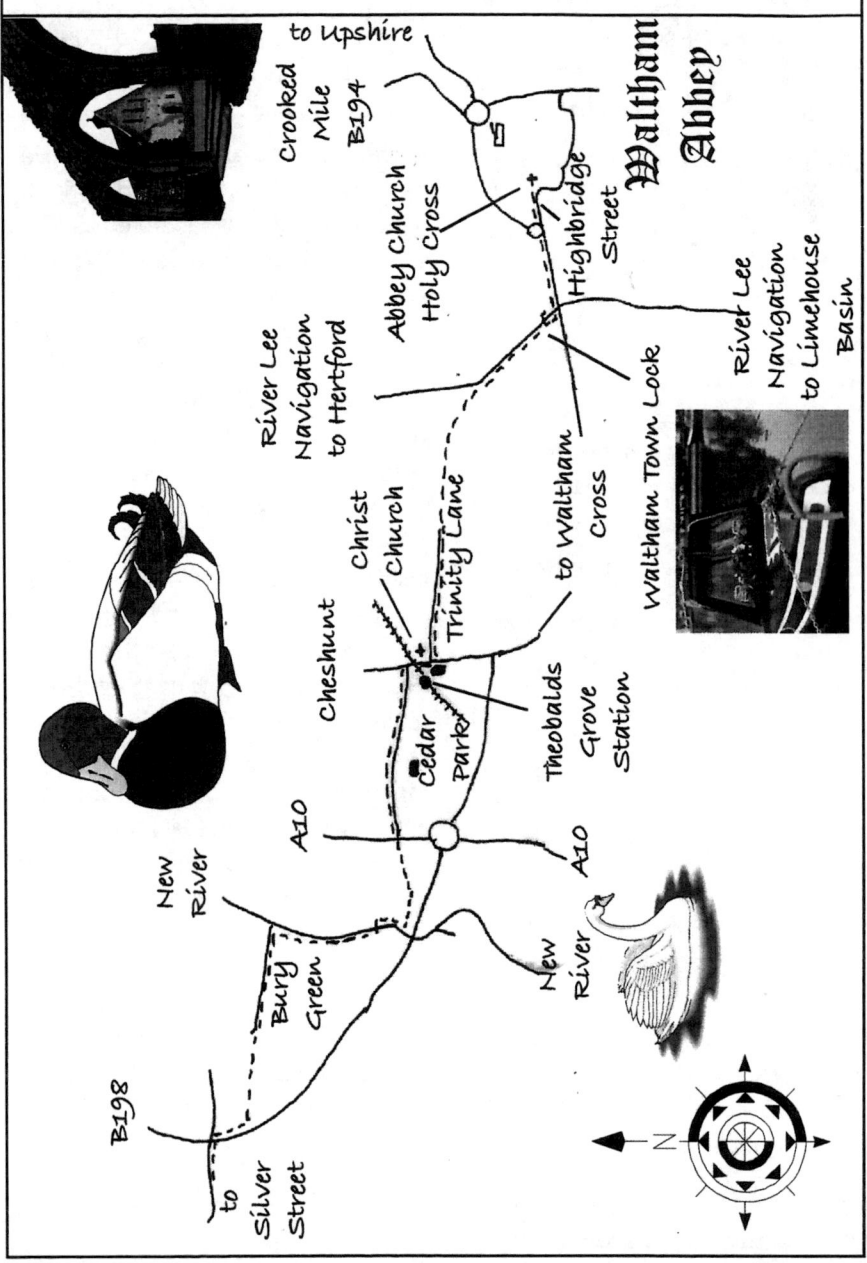

Stage One - WALTHAM ABBEY TO BURY GREEN - 4 MILES - allow 1 1/2 hours.

Basic route - Waltham Abbey - River Lee Navigation - Cheshunt - Theobalds Grove Station - A10 - New River - Bury Green - B198 road bridge.

Map - O.S. Explorer Series No. 174 - Epping Forest & Lee Valley.

Inns - The Wheatsheaf, Theobalds Grove.

Cafe - McDonald's, Waltham Abbey. Cedar Park.

ABOUT THE STAGE - Soon after leaving the Abbey, you walk a short section of the River Lee Navigation before following a path into Cheshunt and Theobalds Grove Station. Next you pass Cedar Park and the site of Theobalds Royal Palace, to the A10. This is the only potentially hazardous road crossing, as there is no footbridge; care is needed. Following paths beyond you reach the New River and follow it for 1/2 mile to Bury Green and onto the B198 road bridge.

WALKING INSTRUCTIONS - From the west door of the cathedral, keep, straight ahead along Highbridge Street, past the Tourist Office on the right and onto the main road to Waltham Cross. Keep to the lefthand side and soon pass McDonald's on the left and cross the road. Continue along the righthand side over the River Lee Navigation and immediately turn right to the towpath. Keep ahead and pass Waltham Town Lock and follow the towpath for some 8 minutes to before the first bridge. Turn left onto a tarmaced path, soon signed Theobalds Grove. Follow the path straight ahead, ignoring all side turnings and reach Trinity Marsh Lane Crossing. Cross the railway line and keep straight ahead along Trinity Lane to the main road, Cheshunt and Theobalds Grove Station opposite; on the left is the Wheatsheaf Inn. On the righthand corner is Christ Church.

Turn right and pass under the railway and immediately left along Theobalds Lane. Keep straight ahead and soon pass Cedar Park on the left. Pass the car park turn and cafe and follow the lane to the A10 road. Cross with care to the middle barrier, turning right along it then left to cross the other carriageway to a path sign beside Rush Lodge. Walk along the track to near the B198 road and keep right, as path signed, to walk along the lefthand side of the field to the New River. Turn right and in a few yards cross a footbridge. Continue with the river on your right for nearly 1/2 mile (10 mins) to a kissing gate and New River Path sign. Turn left into Bury Green and Tudor Avenue and keep straight ahead along it. At the end continue ahead, now on a path along Grove Path to Portland Drive. Turn left and then right along Woodside Close. At No. 2 keep right, as path signed - Barrow Lane - and pass a cemetery on the right. At the end, close to the B198, turn right to the road. Turn left and cross the bridge over the B198, with Crescent Nurseries on the right.

Waltham Town Lock - River Lee Navigation.

RIVER LEE NAVIGATION - Length - Limehouse Basin, Bow to Hertford - 27 3/4 miles. 19 locks.

The River Lee has been, since Roman times, an important trade route to London. An Act of 1571 for an artificial cut was made to help speed up the traffic. At the same time a pound at Waltham Abbey with lock gates - a similar principal to today - was made and is one of the earliest in the country. During the 18th and 19th. century the navigation was improved, these included in 1769 the Waltham, Edmonton and Hackney Cuts (avoiding the River Lee) and pound locks was opened. In 1911 The Lee Conservancy bought the River Stort Navigation and improved it together with the River Lee. By 1930, 130 ton boats could reach Enfield and 100 ton boats to Ware and Hertford. During the rest of the 20th. century many improvements were made including mechanised locks. Whilst many of the locks vary in size the majority are - 85 ft long by 16 ft wide and between 5 and 7 feet deep. Upto Enfield Lock they are double locks and beyond to Hertford, single locks. The river can be either spelt Lee or Lea.

CEDAR PARK - The park is the site of the Royal Palace of Theobalds, originally built about 1563 by Lord Burleigh, Secretary of State, Lord High Treasurer and Master of Requests to Queen Elizabeth Ist; who often visited here. Upon Lord Burleigh death in 1598, his son, Sir Robert Cecil (became the first Earl of Salisbury and the King's first Minister) took over and in 1603, he entertained James the First here. The king liked Theobalds and swapped it for Hatfield House in 1607; thereby becoming a Royal Palace. It was here that James 1st. died in 1625 and Charles 1st. who had been brought up here, became King. Later Charles 1st. rode from here to Nottingham and raised his standard at the Civil War. He later lost to the Parliamentarians and was executed. His property was seized and ransacked and sold off. By 1783 the property was described "as ruinous". In 1920 the area was given to the Cheshunt Council. The main entrance gates, which you pass, has plaques and coats of arms on showing its history. over the last 450 years. The park is most attractive and part of the ruins can still be seen; there is also a cafe. Hatfield House is still owned today by the Cecil family and is a particularly fine Jacobean House. Queen Elizabeth the First was brought up here.

For nearly a century the Temple Bar gate stood in the grounds, being bought by Sir Henry Meux, a wealthy brewer and a former owner of Theobalds. The Temple Bar Inn in Cheshunt still recalls its name. In 2004 it was removed and rebuilt beside St. Paul's Cathedral, being the last remaining 17th. century (1672) gate into the city.

The New River, near Bury Green.

NEW RIVER - Originally built by Sir Hugh Myddleton, a Welsh Engineer, in 1609 -1613, to bring clear water to London. At first it was 40 miles long but today only 23 miles remain and is still used by Thames Water Board; the river being fed by springs and the River Lee near Hertford.

Follow the Countryside Code.

* Be safe - plan ahead and follow any signs.

* Leave gates and property as you find them.

* Protect plants and animals, and take your litter home.

* Keep dogs under close control.

* Consider other people.

Stage Two -
BURY GREEN TO NORTHAW
- 5 MILES

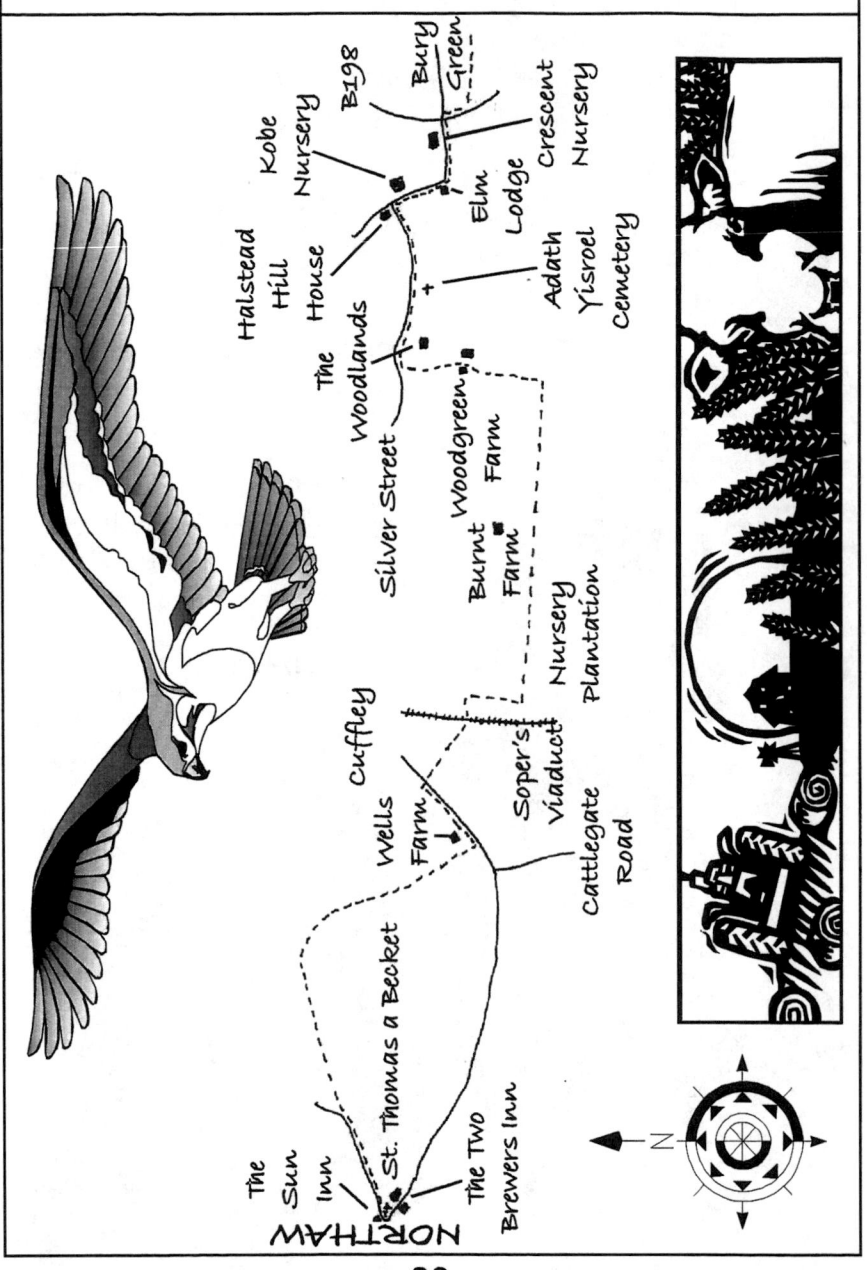

Stage Two - Bury Green to Northaw - 5 miles - allow 2 hours.

Basic route - B198 - Crescent Nursery - Kobe Nursery - Silver Street - Woodgreen Farm - Chain Walk - Nursery Plantation - Soper's Viaduct - B156 - Northaw Brook - Hemps Hill - Vineyards Road - Northaw.

Maps - O.S. Explorer Series Nos -
- 174 - Epping Forest & Lee Valley.
- 182 - St. Albans & Hatfield.

Inns - The Sun Inn and The Two Brewers Inn, Northaw.

ABOUT THE STAGE - After passing a couple of nurseries on a quiet lane you follow delightful tracks beside woodland with views to central London at first. You descend gently to Northaw Brook and the impressive Soper's Viaduct (railway), before gaining the B156 road. After a short road walk you are once more back in fields as you curve round and ascend Hemps Hill to the Northaw Road. A short distance along here you reach the attractive green, church and inns of Northaw.

WALKING INSTRUCTIONS - Cross the road bridge over the B198 and pass Crescent Nursery on your right. In 300 yards the road turns sharp right with Elm Lodge on the left. Continue on the road past Hazelmere House on the left and Kobe Nursery and house on the right. Immediately, turn left on Silver Street and follow the road down and up past Woodgreen Park and Adath Yisroel Cemetery (Jewish), on your left. Pass the drive to The Woodlands on your left and just after, as path signed, turn left along the track/drive to Woodgreen Farm - a horse riding complex. Bear slightly right between the buildings, still on a track, and follow it along righthand side of the field to a junction. Here, as path signed - Northaw 3 miles - turn right to continue on a tree lined track. At first you have view to your left - southwards - to central

London and its skyline of Post Office Tower, Gherkin and London Eye are clearly visible.

Keep straight ahead for nearly two miles on the track, and after 3/4 mile cross a track way crossroads, just south of Burnt Farm. Soon after you have views ahead to Northaw and the church tower stands out prominently - your destination. Later the track becomes most pleasant beside Nursery Plantation on your left and the Soper's Viaduct ahead. Follow the track sharp right and where it turns left for the Viaduct, keep ahead and cross Northaw Brook and ascend the field on a well defined path for 5 mins. before following it left to walk through Soper's Bridge. Keep straight ahead on a hedged track to the B156 road on the fringe of Cuffley.

Soper's Viaduct.

Turn left and pass North Cuffley Lawn Tennis Club on your left. Soon afterwards pass Wells Farm on the right and just after, as path signed - Northaw - 1 1/4 miles - Turn right onto a track with a branch of the Northaw Brook on your right. On your left is the Northaw "Race Course". In 2006 the races were cancelled due to the hardness of the ground! In 1/2 mile keep the hedge on your right and some 15 mins. from the road turn right and left. The path on the right goes uphill to Cuffley. Continue with the brook on your left and a fence on your right, as you follow the path. In 200 yards turn left - ahead can be seen Thornton's Farm. Ascend the path with a fence on your left to a kissing gate and onto another, as you follow the tree lined path over Hemps Hill to a kissing gate and the Northaw Road - Vineyards Road. Turn left along the road past houses on your left and woodland on your right. Pass Northaw Primary School on the right before reaching Northaw church, green, and the Sun Inn; the Two Brewers Inn is just beyond the church.

Northaw church and pinnacle from earlier church.

NORTHAW - Church dedicated to St. Thomas a Becket of Canterbury.
The manor is one of 34 once held by the Abbey of St. Albans, and originally given by King Offa of Mercia. The present church is the third one on this site and was built in 1882, and is a very pleasant example of Victorian Gothic, with mosaic's inside. The font is from the earlier church and dates from the 15th. century. The second church was built in 1809 but only survived 71 years, when it was destroyed by fire in February 1881. Beside the tower base can be seen two pinnacles which came from the earlier church.

Northaw is a particularly attractive village and as the sign on the green states, has been a winner in the *"Best Kept Small Village"* in Hertfordshire competition. The village in the past has not been so quiet for Alice (bastard daughter) was murdered by Thomas Hurry and Alice Andrew on December 1st. 1751. They were hung on March 18th. 1752 for their crime.

Stage Three -
NORTHAW TO NORTH MYMMS
- 6 MILES

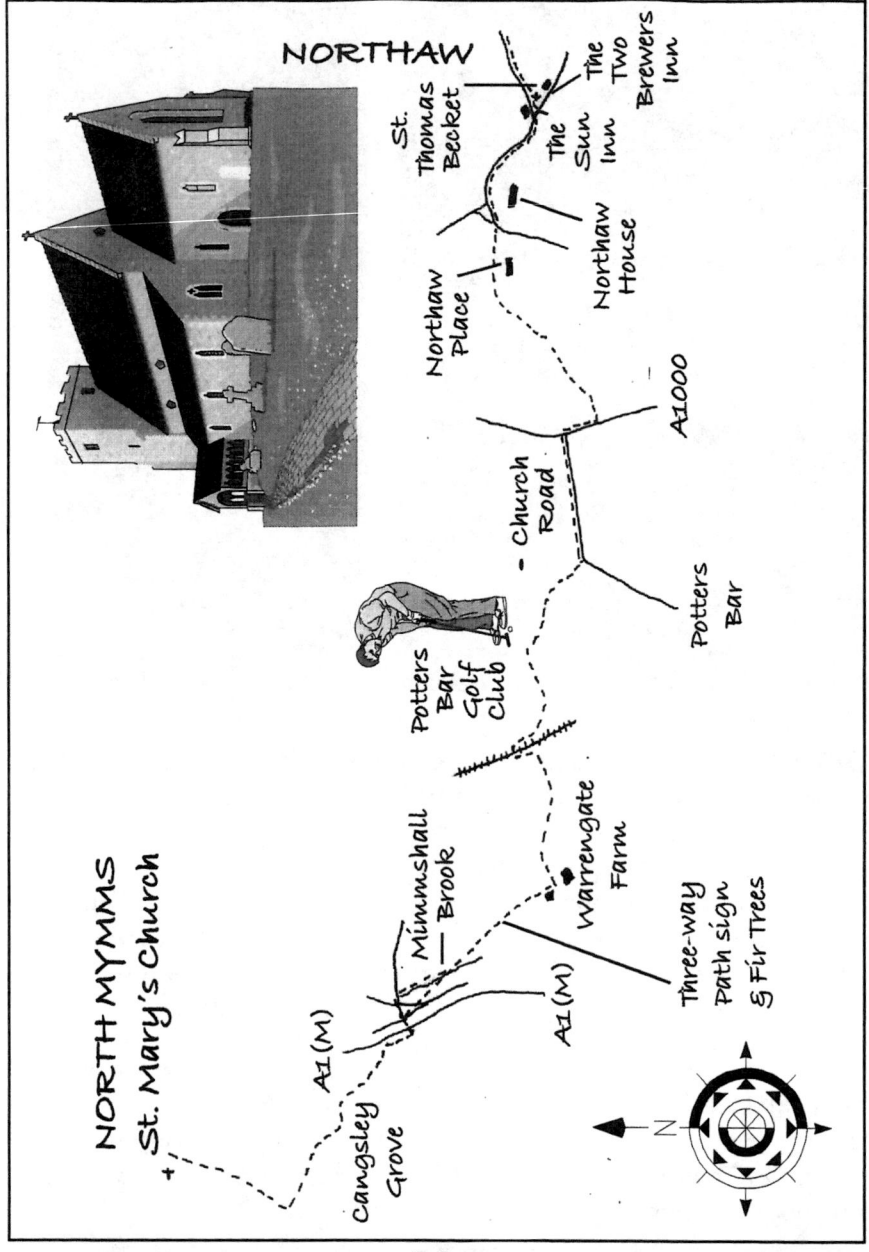

Stage Three - NORTHAW TO NORTH MYMMS - 6 MILES
- allow 2 1/4 hours.

Basic route - Northaw House - Northaw Place - Potters Bar - Potters Bar Golf Course - Furzefield Wood - Warrengate Bungalows - Mimmshaft Brook - M1 - Cangsley Grove - North Mymms, St. Mary's church.

Map - O.S. 1:25,000 Explorer Series No. 182 - St. Albans & Hatfield.

Shop - Post Office/Shop, Church Road, Potters Bar.

ABOUT THE STAGE - After passing two imposing "halls" in Northaw, you cross the northern end of Potters Bar, passing a shop the only amenity on this stage. After this you cross fields and woodland on paths and tracks to the magnificent and complete 14th. century church at North Mymms. Here you are almost two thirds of the way to St. Albans!

WALKING INSTRUCTIONS - From The Green, turn right along Judge's Hill, passing The Sun Inn on the right and soon after on the right, Northaw Pond. Follow the road right before curving left with the white painted Northaw House to your left. Ignore the first road on your right and a short distance later at the second one go straight across to the path, signed - Coopers Lane. Keep to the righthand edge of the field with Northaw Place on your left. Follow the path left at the end of the field keeping the fence on your right and later on your left to the end of woodland. Cross a footbridge and keep to the lefthand side of the wood to its next corner and a kissing gate. Bear half right across the field to a stile in the far righthand corner. Continue ahead to walk beside houses to a kissing gate on your right. Turn right through it and walk past garages and houses of Norman Court to the Great North Road, A1000.

The Green and The Sun Inn, Northaw.

Turn right and pass a white post, with London insignia - 24 Vict - a toll point for bringing in coal to London. You will pass another one on the next road. A few yards later turn left along Church Road. Pass the Post Office/Shop on the left and Mount Grace School. Where the road turn sharp left - Potters Bar Station is little over 1/2 mile away down this road - keep ahead into Mountway by a footpath sign. Where the road turns left at a solitary oak tree, turn right and left as path signed, to follow a path with houses on your left. You soon reach Potters Bar Golf Club course. The right of way is well signed with path posts and keeps beside a small stream on your left. Follow the path left then right still with a stream on your left to the railway embankment. Keep right beside to a tunnel on your left. Walk through and turn left beside an industrial estate to where the road turns right. Here on the right is path sign No. 15. Walk past more industrial units to a road and turn right. Immediately pass access into Furzefield Wood - a local nature reserve. Just after cross a bridge over a stream and turn left onto a path beside the stream on your left. Follow it for nearly 1/2 mile (10 mins.) to opposite Warrengate Farm.

London Coal Boundary Marker.

Turn right and pass Warrengate Bungalows on your left. Continue along the righthand edge of the field beside a hedge and in 8 mins reach a small group of fir trees and a 3-way path post. In mid July the field was full of rape seed, and although the path was defined; it was hard work. At the path sign keep straight ahead, on Path No. 12 and descend to Mimmshall Brook. Turn right and keep along the field edge with the brook on your left to a stile and Hawkshead Lane. Turn left to a cross roads and go straight across to the next road, immediately before the A1(M). Cross to a footbridge and cross over the A1(M). Over, turn right, first keeping close to the motorway before bearing left on the track - Public Byway No. 5. Keep straight ahead and ignore another path on your right and reach after 1/2 mile from the motorway a path cross roads. Go straight across and soon reach a gate and woodland on your immediate left - Cangsley Grove. Continue to another gate and path/track T junction. Turn right and follow a track with Walsingham Wood and North Mymms Park, well to your left. The track becomes tarmaced and at Church Cottage turn left to St. Mary's church - path signed - Tollgate Road 1/2 mile & Colney Heath 1 1/4 miles - both your destinations on stage four.

The posts date back to time when coal or wine entering London was taxed; it all started in the 17th. century and the money was used to help rebuild London, following the Great Fire of 1666. The posts have the Corporation of London's coat of arms - a shield with the cross of St. George and a sword in one quater. The mark 24 Vic refers to Queen Victoria's reign - 1837 onwards; hence the post's date is 1861.

NORTHAW HOUSE - Built in 1698 with the north front (seen from the road) with five bays and a three bay pediment. In the early 19th. century the house was enlarged to seven bays and additional rooms. The semicircular porch is late 18th. century style.

NORTHAW PLACE - Built in c.1690 by Sir George Hutchins, who was the King's Serjeant (Barrister of the highest rank) and one of the Commissioners of the Great Seal 1690-3. In the 18th. century the building was made three storeys high, instead of two and an attic. One bedroom has late 17th. century panel paintings in Chinese style and reputed to be the work of Robert Robinson.

NORTH MYMMS PARK - Considered one of the best examples of late Elizabethan style in Hertfordshire. Built by Sir Ralph Coningsby (Sheriff) in 1596 at a cost of £10,000. Originally built as a courtyard house but later made into a H plan. The entrance hall has a French chimney piece dated 1515 and another 1563, would appear to be from another property. The north front is two storeys high. Between 1716-1799 the house was owned by the Duke's of Leeds. The gardens were designed by Sir Ernest George. The rose garden is the work of William Robinson, a noted reformer of the English garden in the later 19th. century.

ST. MARY'S CHURCH, NORTH MYMMS PARK - The chancel of the 13th. century is the earliest part, with the nave and aisles dated c.1340. The west tower is 15th. century. It is a most complete and unspoilt 14th. century church, which despite its remote location still attracts a strong congregation of some 100 people each Sunday. There are several impressive memorials and brasses. The brass of William de Kesterne, Vicar - 1344 - 1361 is particularly fine. In the north aisle is the Beresford Tomb, made at the end of the 16th. century from Derbyshire alabaster, and a memorial to two sisters who died in 1584. Perhaps the finest monument is the Somers Memorial, made in 1716 by Peter Scheemakers. It is unusual in having a marble door leading into the vestry. Lord Somers, who lived in the parish at Brookmans, was Lord Chancellor of England during the reign of King William and Mary. There is much to see here and a walk around the church and churchyard will bring you to many interesting features, including a tomb shaped like a tea caddy to the Gaussen family.

Somers Memorial and the Kesteven Brass, on the left.

Stage Four -
NORTH MYMMS TO TYTTENHANGER
- 4 1/2 MILES

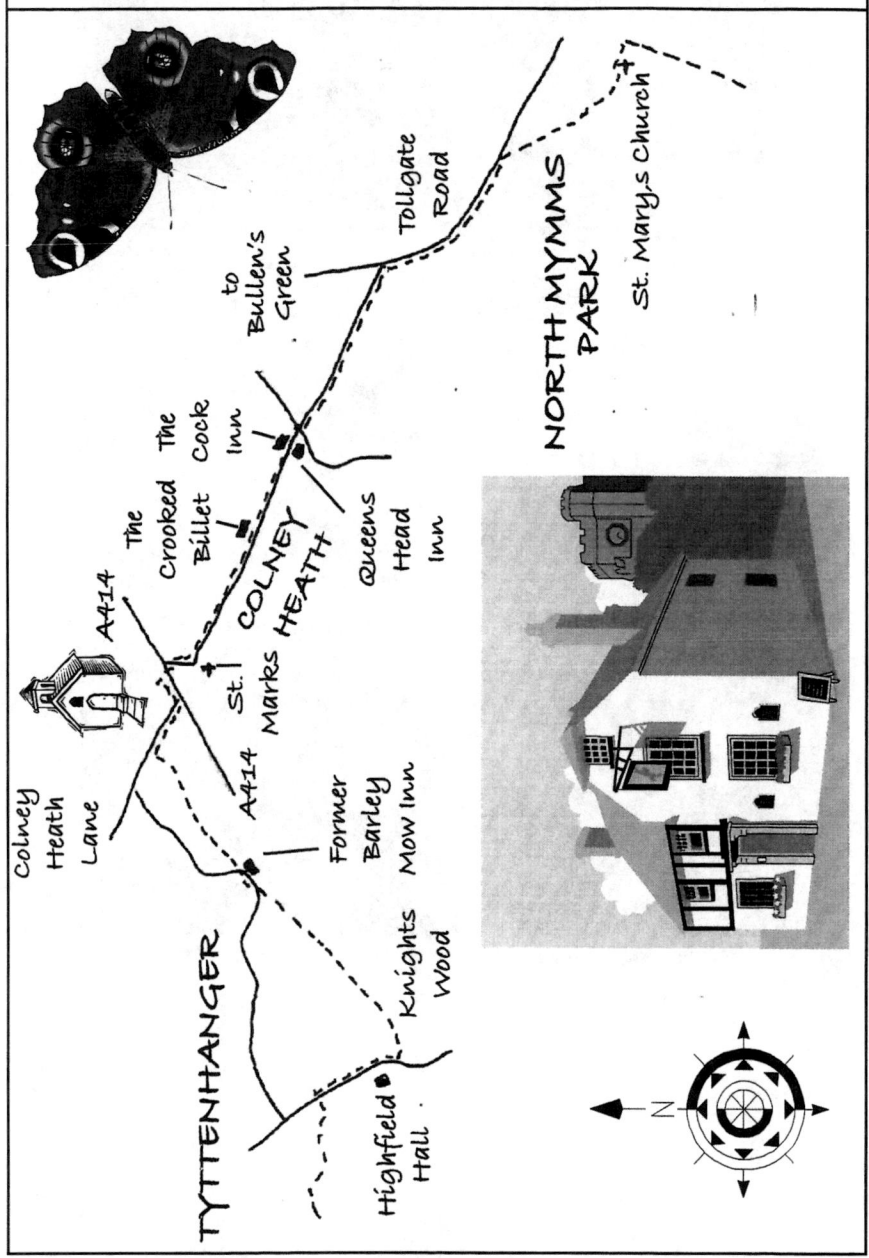

Stage Four - NORTH MYMMS TO TYTTENHANGER - 4 1/2 miles - allow 1 1/2 hours.

Basic Route - North Mymms Church - North Mymms Park - Tollgate Road - Colney Heath - A414 - Former Barley Mow Inn - Knights Wood - Highfield Hall, Tyttenhanger.

Map - O.S. 1:25,000 Explorer Series No. 182 - St. Albans and Hadfield.

Inns - Queens Head, The Cock and The Crooked Billet - Colney Heath.

Shop - Colney Heath.

ABOUT THE STAGE - Leaving the church you cross North Mymms Park with views of the Elizabethan house before reaching Tollgate Road. This leads you to Colney Heath and your first shop and inns for eight miles. After crossing the A414 footbridge, you follow paths to Tyttenhanger on the edge of St. Albans, ready for the final stage.

WALKING INSTRUCTIONS - From the church tower descend to a kissing gate and into North Mymms Park. Bear slightly right and cross the park to a footbridge with trees to your right. Keep ahead - no path line - aiming for the far righthand corner of the parkland field to a stile and Tollgate Road. Turn left and after 1/2 mile turn left along the first road into Colney Heath. Reaching a cross roads with the Queens Head on the left and The Cock Inn on the right, keep straight ahead through Colney Heath, passing the shop and later The Crooked Billet Inn. At the end of the village the road bears right with St. Marks church, built in 1845, on the left. Follow the road to the A414 - North Orbital Road - and turn left to cross it via the footbridge. Descend left and take the first road on your right - Colney Heath Lane.

In less than 5 mins. (1/4 mile) along the lane you will see a path sign on your right. On your left is a stile. This path to the former Barley Mow Inn, appears little used and if overgrown you can road walk round by continuing on the road and turning left along the lane to the former inn. Over the stile bear left and immediately right towards the hedge in the middle of the field. Keep straight ahead with the hedge on your left to a footbridge and onto the road beside the Barley Mow. Turn left and pass the former inn to a road just after and a path sign and stile. Keep straight ahead on the path, paralleling the A414 for 1/4 mile to your left. First keep the lane on your right before crossing the field to a footbridge. Continue ahead now on a hedged path and pass Knights Wood on your left and a grass track with path sign - Highfield Lane 1/4 mile. Continue to the lane and turn right, passing Highfield Hall on your left. Just after pass Highfield Farm in the hamlet of Tyttenhanger, and a few yards later, left onto a hedged track - path signed Nightingale Lane 1/2 mile.

COLNEY HEATH - A popular haunt for Highwaymen and where prize fights and cock fighting took place; the Cock Inn recalls this activity.

TYTTENHANGER - part of the heath - Colney Heath - formerly owned by St. Albans Abbey until the dissolution of the monasteries. The former Barley Mow Inn used to brew its own beer.

Church Cottage, North Mymms.

North Mymms Church, dedicated to St. Mary.

Stage Five -
TYTTENHANGER TO ST. ALBANS CATHEDRAL - 4 1/2 MILES

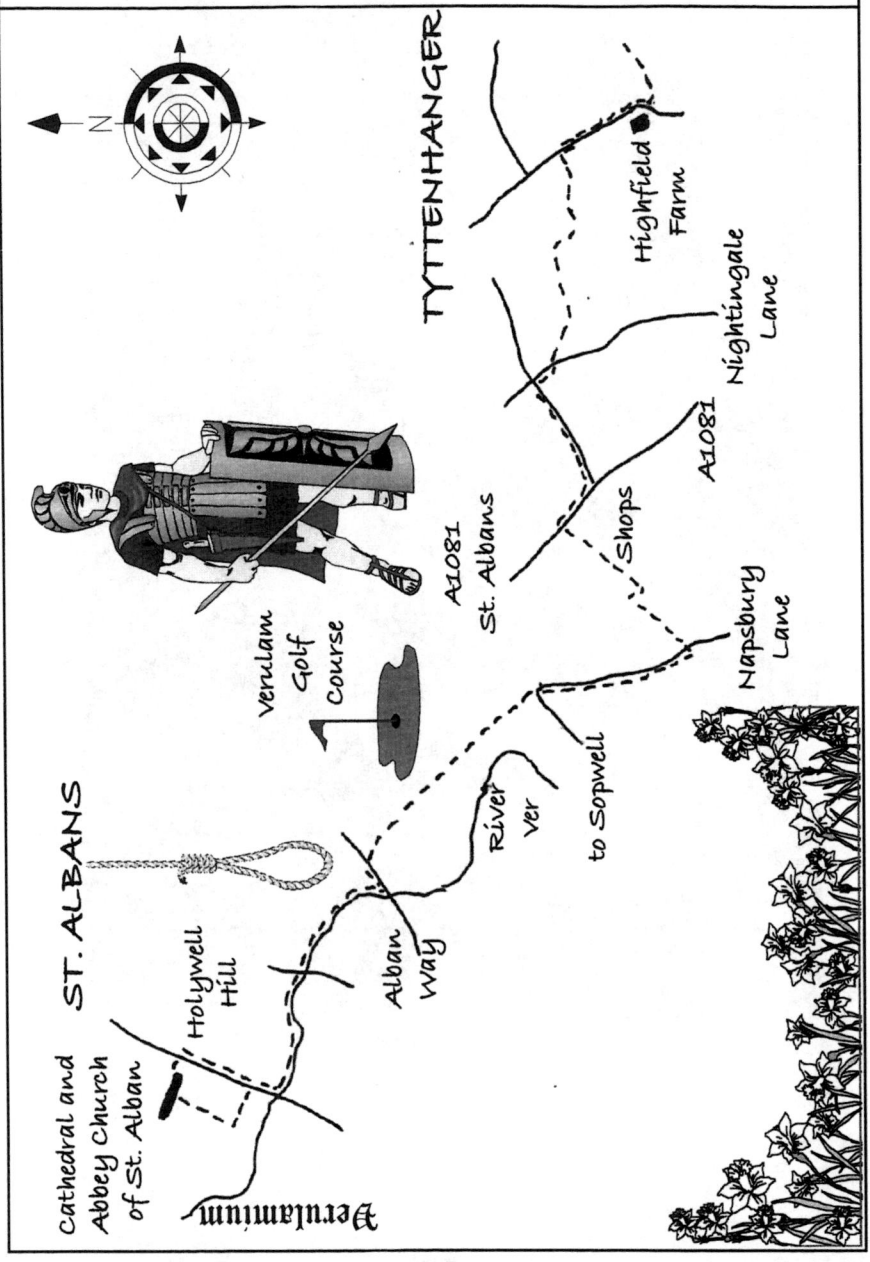

N

TYTTENHANGER

Highfield Farm

Nightingale Lane

A1081

A1081 St. Albans

Shops

Napsbury Lane

Verulam Golf Course

to Sopwell

River Ver

Alban Way

ST. ALBANS

Holywell Hill

Cathedral and Abbey Church of St. Alban

Verulamium

Stage Five - TYTTENHANGER TO ST. ALBANS CATHEDRAL - 4 1/2 miles - allow 1 1/2 hours.

Basic Route - Highfield Hall, Tyttenhanger - Nightingale Lane - A1081 - Napsbury Lane - Colne Valley Walk - A5183 - Verulam Golf Course - The Alban Way - St. Albans Cathedral.

Map - O.S. 1:25,000 Explorer Series No. 182 - St. Albans and Hadfield.

Inns - Numerous in St. Albans.

Cafe - Numerous in St. Albans.

Shop - Near Herons Way.

ABOUT THE STAGE - Good paths lead you around the south and western side of St. Albans to the cathedral. Apart from a shop just off the route at Heron's Way, there are no facilities until St. Albans, which has everything.

WALKING INSTRUCTIONS - Turn left along the hedged track/path - Nightingale lane - 1/2 mile. Follow it right then left to the lane, in about 10 mins. Turn right to a road and left along it to the A1081. Cross and turn right and in 5 mins, turn left at path sign - No. 58 - Herons Way. At the first road, cross, but to your left is a small shopping centre. Keep ahead on the path which turn right then left to Napsbury Lane. Turn right over the railway line and in 8 mins turn left - for Sopwell - and turn right immediately, as path signed - Alban Way and Riverside Path - 1/2 mile. Keep straight ahead on the path with the River Ver well to your left, as you walk through the Verulam Golf Course. At the end ascend to the former railway line - Alban Way - and turn right (south-westwards).

After 4 mins and immediately after crossing above the River Ver, turn right and descend steps - signposted - Abbey 1 mile - not far to go now! Continue by the river and in 8 mins cross a road and continue near the river to your next road, Holywell Hill; now you can see the cathedral!

Turn right and in a few yards left before the Duke of Marlborough Inn, into Grove Road. Follow it round to your right and just before the entrance to The Abbey Primary School, turn left into Lady Spencer Grove. Follow the path to open space and turn right and ascend to the west door of the cathedral. After your visit turn right and walk past the cathedral to the top of Holywell Hill and turn left to the main shopping area and Tourist Information Centre.

Railway Stations - The Abbey Railway Station is back down Holywell Hill. The main railway station, take the second road on your right.

HOLYWELL HILL - Just up from where you turn left on the right is Belmont Hill, the corner of Torrington House grounds. A plaque here states -

> "Near here stood Holywell House,
> Favourite residence of the
> Duke of Marlborough
> 1650 - 1720
> and his wife
> Sarah Churchill."

Torrington House - *"Eleanor Hare Omerod lived here - 1887 - 1901."*

Also on Holywell Hill was a Pilgrims Rest Inn - now gone, alas!

ABBEY GATEHOUSE - As you ascend to the cathedral on your left is massive Abbey Gatehouse, built in the 1360's. Inside in 1479 the third printing press in England is believed to have been here. Following the dissolution of the Monasteries, between 1553 - 1869 - the gatehouse served as the local prison. In 1871 it became part of St. Albans School.

The West entrance to the cathedral and Abbey Church of St. Alban.

A LITTLE ABOUT THE CATHEDRAL AND ABBEY CHURCH OF ST. ALBANS -

ST ALBAN - In the 3rd. century in the Roman city of Verulamium, named after the River Ver, - just down the "hill" from the cathedral, lived a Roman soldier who gave shelter to a Christian priest - Amphibalus - the word means cloak. The Roman, although a worshipper of Roman gods, was receptive to the Christian faith. When the authorities learnt that a Christian was hiding here, Alban donned the priests clothes and allowed him to escape. Later Alban was arrested and he proclaimed the Christian faith, whereupon he was flogged and again refused to denounce his faith. He was sentenced to death and taken across the River Ver to the top of the hill and had his head cut off. According to legend, a fountain of water rose from the hill and the original executioner refused to do it. His replacement cut Albans head off and his eyes dropped out! The date is believed to be June 22nd. 209 AD.

Alban was England's first Christian martyr (a layman, not a priest) and the site soon became a major pilgrimage centre, of both England and Europe, where the sick were healed and miracles took place. During the Middle Ages, every English King and Queen made the pilgrimage, and Kings Edward 1st., Edward 2nd., and Richard 2nd. were particularly devoted to the shrine. Over time St. Albans Abbey became the major abbey of England. Inside are shrines to both Amphibalus and St. Alban.

CATHEDRAL AND ABBEY CHURCH OF ST. ALBAN - In 793 A.D. a Benedictine monastery was founded on the site. Nearly 300 years later between 1077 - 1115, Paul of Caen began building the Abbey using flint and Roman bricks from the nearby Roman town of Verulamium. At the time of the dissolution of the monasteries by Henry 8th. in 1539 the abbey became the largest parish church in England. Most of the abbey's buildings were destroyed and only the gatehouse and present building survive. It wasn't until 1877 that it became a cathedral.

The outside may not be so attractive, mostly due to Hertfordshire's lack of stone, with flint and Roman bricks used instead, there is considerable amount of the original Norman building remaining, especially the Great Crossing Tower. The whole building is still huge and very large for its population; but luckily it has survived. The principal feature is the shrine of St. Alban, carved from Purbeck marble in 1308. This was rebuilt from 2,000 fragments in the 19th. century and recently topped with a red canopy, embroidered with flowers that Alban would have seen as he ascended to his execution. Here pilgrims have gathered for over 1,700 years. On St. Albans day in late June there are services where each member of the congregation lay a red rose on his shrine,

The Wallingford Screen - 15th. century.

and a procession. In 2006, the celebrations were joined by the Archbishop of Canterbury.

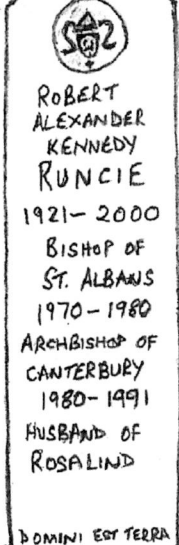

ROBERT
ALEXANDER
KENNEDY
RUNCIE
1921 - 2000
BISHOP OF
ST. ALBANS
1970 - 1980
ARCHBISHOP OF
CANTERBURY
1980 - 1991
HUSBAND OF
ROSALIND

DOMINI EST TERRA

Among the places of special interest inside, are the medieval wall paintings; one is to St. James, with his staff and scalloped shell clearly visible - pilgrim saint of Spain and one of the world's most popular pilgrimages to his shrine at Santiago de Compostela in N. W. Spain. The Wallingford screen dating to the late 15th. century. The 14th. century Lady Chapel and the Ramryge Chapel, after the Abbot Ramryge, built in 1522.

Outside on the northern side can be seen the graves to many people associated with the cathedral, and especially to Robert Runcie who became Bishop of St. Albans and later Archbishop of Canterbury. Beyond the west front is the large gate house.

St. Albans Cathedral - west front and tower.

If time permits you can explore the Romans remains and museum in nearby Verulamium Park.

St. Albans has much more to see and explore and of particular note to complete the story is the Clock Tower in the High Street. Built between 1403-1412, it is the only medieval clock tower in England. You can ascend 93 steps to the top for a view of the city and cathedral. In front of the tower stood an Eleanor Cross, demolished in the 18th. century.

ST. ALBANS WAY WALK LOG

Date started ....

Date completed ....

Route point	Mile No.	Time	Comments
Waltham Abbey	0		
Waltham Town Lock	1/2		
Theobalds Grove	2		
New River	3		
B198 Bridge	4		
Woodgreen Farm	5		
Sopers Viaduct	7 1/2		
Northaw	9		
A1000	11		
Warrengate Farm	13		
North Mymms	15		
Colney Heath	17 1/2		
Tyttenhanger	20		
A1081	21 1/2		
Napsbury Lane	22		
Verulam Golf Course	23		
Alban Way	24		
St. Albans Cathedral	25		
Railway Station	26		

The mileage for each place
is for guide purposes only.

THE PILGRIM WAYS WALK BADGE

Complete the pilgrimage in this book and get the above special embroidered badge and signed certificate.
Badges are blue cloth with shell and lettering in yellow.

BADGE & CERTIFICATE ORDER FORM

Date walk completed..

NAME ....

ADDRESS ....

....

Price: £6.00 each including postage, packing, VAT and signed completion certificate. Amount enclosed (Payable to The John Merrill Foundation) ..
From:
The John Merrill Foundation, 32, Holmesdale, Waltham Cross, Hertfordshire. EN8 8QY

HAPPY WALKING T SHIRT - £7.50 inc. p & p.
Fax +44(0)870 131 5061
e-mail - marathonhiker@aol.com
********** YOU MAY PHOTOCOPY THIS FORM **********

WHY I GO ON A PILGRIMAGE

For me an able bodied person making a pilgrimage does so on his two feet, carrying the bear necessities of life on his back, and walking the whole way there. Today, the term pilgrimage, has a variety of meaning, as most come by car or coach, not just to Walsingham but to the other major pilgrim centres of Santiago de Compostela, Fatima, Rome, Lourdes and Trondheim. The actual walking pilgrim is a bit of a rarity, but he is the true one, who has laboured many days through hardship to arrive at the shrine, to make his or her spiritual commitment. Not that I am decrying other peoples efforts. All I am trying to say, is that a pilgrim who has walked has seen so much and prepared himself as he walked and is ready and 'cleansed" for the shrine.

I believe it should be done alone, for although other people's friendship on the walk is enjoyable it lessens the impact the journey has on the mind. With someone else the hardship is lessened and the places seen and explored are not taken in with the same force as when one is alone. Walking alone enables you have a profound deep experience which if shared is halved. By walking alone you discover the places enroute and you never forget what you have seen and experienced. Also, being on your own means that "special" things will happen to you, which if you were in a group would just not materialise.

I have made many pilgrimages but I do not consider myself religious more a spiritual person. I was brought up a Christian but at the age of thirteen went to a Quaker boarding school. There I went to their meeting houses and experienced their peaceful approach to religion. After that I attended church services infrequently but always had a deep faith in God. On every marathon walk I know I am guided and my angel is beside me, and have never experienced any mishap. In every village or town I come to I always visit the church, for it is the open bible of the area and a place to give thanks for getting this far. I have been to India and Nepal many times and have studied the Buddhist faith. Whilst there is much that I agree with and know the power of meditation, they don't believe in God, but I do believe in reincarnation!

On my pilgrimage from King's Lynn to Walsingham, I know as I was "looked after" and my guardian angel ensured I did not put a foot wrong. Although I had sore feet, they never bothered me and I was in high spirits and at peace. I followed tracks, paths and minor roads to Walsingham. Arriving at Pilgrim's House, I felt I had arrived home. In the morning I walked to the Slipper Chapel to make my prayers and light a candle. I walked back along the "Pilgrim's walk" - the Holy Mile - to Walsingham and onto the shrine of Our Lady of Walsingham. After this I explored the church and ruined priory before catching the bus and train back to Ely. I returned content and at peace.

Catholic, Slipper Chapel, Pilgrim badge, Walsingham, Norfolk, England.

THE PILGRIM'S WAY SERIES by Revd. John N. Merrill

THE WALSINGHAM WAY - Ely to Walsingham - 72 miles - .£8.95
- 56 pages and 40 photographs.

THE WALSINGHAM WAY - King's Lynn to Walsingham - 35 miles - £9.95
- 72 pages and 50 colour photographs.

THE WALSINGHAM WAY - 77 miles - Bury St. Edmunds to Walsingham....£9.95

TURN LEFT AT GRANJA DE LA MORERUELA - 700 miles - Seville to Santiago de Compostela, Spain. 1-903627 - 40 - 0 ....£14.95.. - 172 pages and 120 photographs

NORTH TO SANTIAGO DE COMPOSTELA VIA FATIMA - 650 miles from Lagos, Algarve, through Portugal via Fatima to Santiago de Compostela.........£17.95.. - 220 pages and 160 photographs

ST. OLAV'S WAY - 400 MILES - NORWAY - Photgraphic book and basic guide ....£12.95 - 124 pages and 130 photographs.

ST. WINEFRIDE'S WAY - 14 miles - St. Asaph to Holywell. 40 pages. 5 maps. 20 photographs.. £6.95

ST. ALBAN'S WAY - 25 mile walk from Waltham Abbey to St. Alban's Cathedral. Linking together two major medieval pilgrimage centres. 48 Pages. 7 maps. 18 colour photographs. £7.95

ST. KENELM'S TRAIL by John Price - From the Clent Hills to Winchcombe Abbey - 60 miles. ISBN 978-0-9553691-6-2 . 60 pages 5 maps....£7.50

DERBYSHIRE PILGRIMAGES - The pilgrimage routes, saints and hermits of the county and Peak District. Plus a St. Bertram Walk and about a pilgrimage.
48 pages. £5.95

LONDON TO ST. ALBANS - 36 MILES ...ISBN 978-0-9560649-7-4
80 pages. Wire bound. 45 photos. 8 maps. A stunning walk from Westminster to St. Albans via 32 churches. £9.95

FOLKESTONE, HYTHE TO CANTERBURY - 25 MILES
ISBN 9780956064981..............68 pages. 40 colour phots. 8 maps. £9.95

LONDON TO CANTERBURY - 75 MILES.
ISBN 9780956064967 140 pages. 146 PHOTOS. 15 maps...................£12.95

LONDON TO WALSINGHAM - 190 MILES
ISBN 9780956464422.................256pages. 250 photos. 40 maps. ...£14.95

THE JOHN SCHORNE PEREGRINATION by Michael Mooney. 27 mile walk in Buckinghamshire to North Marston, the site of medieval miracles and pilgrimage.
A5. 56 pages. 16 colour photographs. 8 maps. £7.95

OTHER BOOKS by Revd. John N. Merrill

CIRCULAR WALK GUIDES -
SHORT CIRCULAR WALKS IN THE PEAK DISTRICT - Vols. 1 to 9
CIRCULAR WALKS IN WESTERN PEAKLAND
SHORT CIRCULAR WALKS IN THE STAFFORDSHIRE MOORLANDS
SHORT CIRCULAR WALKS - TOWNS & VILLAGES OF THE PEAK DISTRICT
SHORT CIRCULAR WALKS AROUND MATLOCK
SHORT CIRCULAR WALKS IN "PEAK PRACTICE COUNTRY."
SHORT CIRCULAR WALKS IN THE DUKERIES
SHORT CIRCULAR WALKS IN SOUTH YORKSHIRE
SHORT CIRCULAR WALKS IN SOUTH DERBYSHIRE
SHORT CIRCULAR WALKS AROUND BUXTON
SHORT CIRCULAR WALKS AROUND WIRKSWORTH
SHORT CIRCULAR WALKS IN THE HOPE VALLEY
40 SHORT CIRCULAR WALKS IN THE PEAK DISTRICT
CIRCULAR WALKS ON KINDER & BLEAKLOW
SHORT CIRCULAR WALKS IN SOUTH NOTTINGHAMSHIRE
SHORT CIRCULAR WALKS IN CHESHIRE
SHORT CIRCULAR WALKS IN WEST YORKSHIRE
WHITE PEAK DISTRICT AIRCRAFT WRECKS
CIRCULAR WALKS IN THE DERBYSHIRE DALES
SHORT CIRCULAR WALKS FROM BAKEWELL
SHORT CIRCULAR WALKS IN LATHKILL DALE
CIRCULAR WALKS IN THE WHITE PEAK
SHORT CIRCULAR WALKS IN EAST DEVON
SHORT CIRCULAR WALKS AROUND HARROGATE
SHORT CIRCULAR WALKS IN CHARNWOOD FOREST
SHORT CIRCULAR WALKS AROUND CHESTERFIELD
SHORT CIRCULAR WALKS IN THE YORKS DALES - Vol 1 - Southern area.
SHORT CIRCULAR WALKS IN THE AMBER VALLEY (Derbyshire)
SHORT CIRCULAR WALKS IN THE LAKE DISTRICT
SHORT CIRCULAR WALKS IN THE NORTH YORKSHIRE MOORS
SHORT CIRCULAR WALKS IN EAST STAFFORDSHIRE
LONG CIRCULAR WALKS IN THE PEAK DISTRICT - Vol.1 to 5.
DARK PEAK AIRCRAFT WRECK WALKS
LONG CIRCULAR WALKS IN THE STAFFORDSHIRE MOORLANDS
LONG CIRCULAR WALKS IN CHESHIRE
WALKING THE TISSINGTON TRAIL
WALKING THE HIGH PEAK TRAIL
WALKING THE MONSAL TRAIL & SETT VALLEY TRAILS
PEAK DISTRICT WALKING - TEN "TEN MILER'S" - Vol 1 and 2.
CLIMB THE PEAKS OF THE PEAK DISTRICT
PEAK DISTRICT WALK A MONTH Vols One,Two, Three, Four, Five & Six
TRAIN TO WALK Vol. One - The Hope Valley Line
DERBYSHIRE LOST VILLAGE WALKS -Vol One and Two.
CIRCULAR WALKS IN DOVEDALE AND THE MANIFOLD VALLEY
CIRCULAR WALKS AROUND GLOSSOP
WALKING THE LONGDENDALE TRAIL
WALKING THE UPPER DON TRAIL
SHORT CIRCULAR WALKS IN CANNOCK CHASE
CIRCULAR WALKS IN THE DERWENT VALLEY
WALKING THE TRAILS OF NORTH-EAST DERBYSHIRE
WALKING THE PENNINE BRIDLEWAY & CIRCULAR WALKS
SHORT CIRCULAR WALKS ON THE NEW RIVER & SOUTH-EAST HERTFORDSHIRE
SHORT CIRCULAR WALKS IN EPPING FOREST
WALKING THE STREETS OF LONDON
LONG CIRCULAR WALKS IN EASTERN HERTFORDSHIRE
LONG CIRCULAR WALKS IN WESTERN HERTFORDSHIRE
WALKS IN THE LONDON BOROUGH OF ENFIELD
WALKS IN THE LONDON BOROUGH OF BARNET
WALKS IN THE LONDON BOROUGH OF HARINGEY
WALK IN THE LONDON BOROUGH OF WALTHAM FOREST
SHORT CIRCULAR WALKS AROUND HERTFORD
THE BIG WALKS OF LONDON
SHORT CIRCULAR WALKS AROUND BISHOP'S STORTFORD
SHORT CIRCULAR WALKS AROUND EPPING DISTRICT
CIRCULAR WALKS IN THE BOROUGH OF BROXBOURNE
LONDON INTERFAITH WALKS - Vol 1 and Vol. 2
LONG CIRCULAR WALKS IN THE NORTH CHILTERNS
SHORT CIRCULAR WALKS IN EASTERN HERTFORDSHIRE
WORCESTERSHIRE VILLAGE WALKS by Des Wright
WARWICKSHIRE VILLAGE WALKS by Des Wright
WALKING AROUND THE ROYAL PARKS OF LONDON
WALKS IN THE LONDON BOROUGH OF CHELSEA AND ROYAL KENSINGTON

CANAL WALKS -
VOL 1 - DERBYSHIRE & NOTTINGHAMSHIRE
VOL 2 - CHESHIRE & STAFFORDSHIRE
VOL 3 - STAFFORDSHIRE
VOL 4 - THE CHESHIRE RING
VOL 5 - THE GRANTHAM CANAL
VOL 6 - SOUTH YORKSHIRE
VOL 7 - THE TRENT & MERSEY CANAL
VOL 8 - WALKING THE DERBY CANAL RING
VOL 9 - WALKING THE LLANGOLLEN CANAL
VOL 10 - CIRCULAR WALKS ON THE CHESTERFIELD CANAL
VOL 11 - CIRCULAR WALKS ON THE CROMFORD CANAL
Vol.13 - SHORT CIRCULAR WALKS ON THE RIVER LEE NAVIGATION -Vol. 1 - North
Vol. 14 - SHORT CIRCULAR WALKS ON THE RIVER STORT NAVIGATION
Vol.15 - SHORT CIRCULAR WALKS ON THE RIVER LEE NAVIGATION - Vol. 2 - South
Vol. 16 - WALKING THE CANALS OF LONDON
Vol 17 - WALKING THE RIVER LEE NAVIGATION
Vol. 20 - SHORT CIRCULAR WALKS IN THE COLNE VALLEY
Vol 21 - THE BLACKWATER & CHELMER NAVIGATION - End to End.
Vol. 22 - NOTTINGHAM'S LOST CANAL by Bernard Chell.
Vol. 23 - WALKING THE RIVER WEY & GODALMING NAVIAGTIONS END TO END
Vol.25 - WALKING THE GRAND UNION CANAL - LONDON TO BIRMINGHAM.

JOHN MERRILL DAY CHALLENGE WALKS
WHITE PEAK CHALLENGE WALK
THE HAPPY HIKER - WHITE PEAK - CHALLENGE WALK
DARK PEAK CHALLENGE WALK
PEAK DISTRICT END TO END WALKS
STAFFORDSHIRE MOORLANDS CHALLENGE WALK

JOHN MERRILL DAY CHALLENGE WALKS

WHITE PEAK CHALLENGE WALK
THE HAPPY HIKER - WHITE PEAK - CHALLENGE WALK No.2
DARK PEAK CHALLENGE WALK
PEAK DISTRICT END TO END WALKS
STAFFORDSHIRE MOORLANDS CHALLENGE WALK
THE LITTLE JOHN CHALLENGE WALK
YORKSHIRE DALES CHALLENGE WALK
NORTH YORKSHIRE MOORS CHALLENGE WALK
LAKELAND CHALLENGE WALK
THE RUTLAND WATER CHALLENGE WALK
MALVERN HILLS CHALLENGE WALK
THE SALTERiS WAY
THE SNOWDON CHALLENGE
CHARNWOOD FOREST CHALLENGE WALK
THREE COUNTIES CHALLENGE WALK (Peak District).
CAL-DER-WENT WALK
THE QUANTOCK WAY
BELVOIR WITCHES CHALLENGE WALK
THE CARNEDDAU CHALLENGE WALK
THE SWEET PEA CHALLENGE WALK
THE LINCOLNSHIRE WOLDS - BLACK DEATH - CHALLENGE WALK
JENNIFER'S CHALLENGE WALK
THE EPPING FOREST CHALLENGE WALK
THE THREE BOROUGH CHALLENGE WALK - NORTH LONDON
THE HERTFORD CHALLENGE WALK
THE BOSHAM CHALLENGE WALK
THE KING JOHN CHALLENGE WALK
THE NORFOLK BROADS CHALLENGE WALK
THE RIVER MIMRAM WALK
THE ISLE OF THANET CHHALENGE WALK
THE EAST DEVON CHALLENGE WALK

INSTRUCTION & RECORD -

HIKE TO BE FIT.....STROLLING WITH JOHN
THE JOHN MERRILL WALK RECORD BOOK
HIKE THE WORLD - John Merrill's guide to walking & Backpacking.

MULTIPLE DAY WALKS -

THE RIVERS'S WAY
PEAK DISTRICT: HIGH LEVEL ROUTE
PEAK DISTRICT MARATHONS
THE LIMEY WAY
THE PEAKLAND WAY
COMPO'S WAY by Alan Hiley
THE BRIGHTON WAY

COAST WALKS & NATIONAL TRAILS -

ISLE OF WIGHT COAST PATH
PEMBROKESHIRE COAST PATH
THE CLEVELAND WAY
WALKING ANGELSEY'S COASTLINE.
WALKING THE COASTLINE OF THE CHANNEL ISLANDS
THE ISLE OF MAN COASTAL PATH - "The Way of the Gull."
A WALK AROUND HAYLING ISLAND
A WALK AROUND THE ISLE OF SHEPPEY
A WALK AROUND THE ISLE OF JERSEY
WALKING AROUND THE ISLANDS OF ESSEX

DERBYSHIRE & PEAK DISTRICT HISTORICAL GUIDES -

A to Z GUIDE OF THE PEAK DISTRICT
DERBYSHIRE INNS - an A to Z guide
HALLS AND CASTLES OF THE PEAK DISTRICT & DERBYSHIRE
TOURING THE PEAK DISTRICT & DERBYSHIRE BY CAR
DERBYSHIRE FOLKLORE
PUNISHMENT IN DERBYSHIRE
CUSTOMS OF THE PEAK DISTRICT & DERBYSHIRE
WINSTER - a souvenir guide
ARKWRIGHT OF CROMFORD
LEGENDS OF DERBYSHIRE
DERBYSHIRE FACTS & RECORDS
TALES FROM THE MINES by Geoffrey Carr
PEAK DISTRICT PLACE NAMES by Martin Spray
DERBYSHIRE THROUGH THE AGES - Vol 1 -DERBYSHIRE IN PREHISTORIC TIMES
SIR JOSEPH PAXTON
FLORENCE NIGHTINGALE
JOHN SMEDLEY
BONNIE PRINCE CHARLIE & 20 mile walk.
THE STORY OF THE EARLS AND DUKES OF DEVONSHIRE

JOHN MERRILL'S MAJOR WALKS -

TURN RIGHT AT LAND'S END
WITH MUSTARD ON MY BACK
TURN RIGHT AT DEATH VALLEY
EMERALD COAST WALK
I CHOSE TO WALK - Why I walk etc.
A WALK IN OHIO - 1,310 miles around the Buckeye Trail.
I AM GUIDED - the story of John's life.

SKETCH BOOKS -

SKETCHES OF THE PEAK DISTRICT

COLOUR BOOK:-

THE PEAK DISTRICT.......something to remember her by.

OVERSEAS GUIDES -

HIKING IN NEW MEXICO - Vol I - The Sandia and Manzano Mountains.
Vol 2 - Hiking "Billy the Kid" Country.
Vol 4 - N.W. area - " Hiking Indian Country."
"WALKING IN DRACULA COUNTRY" - Romania.
WALKING THE TRAILS OF THE HONG KONG ISLANDS.

VISITOR GUIDES - MATLOCK . BAKEWELL. ASHBOURNE.

See all my books on -
www.johnmerrillwalkguides.co.uk

Pilgrim guides -
www.thejohnmerrillministry.co.uk

Illustrated lectures by John N. Merrill

Lectures on his major walks are available. For further information and bookings, write to John Merrill at

THE JOHN MERRILL FOUNDATION
32, Holmesdale,
Waltham Cross,
Hertfordshire
EN8 8QY
England

Tel/Fax 01992 - 762776
e-mail - marathonhiker@aol.com
www.johnmerrillwalkguides.com

Illustrated Lectures include -

" **WALKING AROUND LONDON**" - a brief look at walking in the city and countryside around London, some 1,800 miles of walking. - Capital Ring, Canals, London Loop, River Thames, New River, Pymmes Brook Trail & Jubilee Walkway, The Wandle Trail, the River Stort and Lee Navigations and Lee Valley Walk.

"**WALKING MY WAY**" - Why I walk and some of walks I have done - a hilarious but exhausting talk, from more than 200,000 miles of walking!

"**LONDON TO WALSINGHAM - 194 MILES - following the medieval pilgrimage route.**

" **LONDON TO CANTERBURY - following the medieval pilgrimage route.**

"**NORTH TO SANTIAGO** via **FATIMA**" - 650 mile pilgrim's walk to Santiago de Compostelo, through Portugal.

"Promoting walking, Pilgrimages, and understanding the countryside."

OTHER NORTH LONDON WALK BOOKS
by JOHN N. MERRILL

SHORT CIRCULAR WALKS ON THE RIVER LEE NAVIGATION - Northern Volume - Ponder's End - Hertford. 64 pages, 23 photographs, 10 detailed maps and walks. History notes.
- ISBN 1-903627-68-0 @ £8.50

WALKING THE RIVER LEE NAVIGATION - VOL 1 & 2.

SHORT CIRCULAR WALKS ON THE NEW RIVER & SOUTH EAST HERTFORDSHIRE
11 walks - 5 to 10 miles long between Waltham Cross and Hertford; many on the New River. New revised and enlarged edition 80 pages, 24 photographs, 13 detailed maps. History notes.
ISBN 1-903627-69-9 @ £8.95

SHORT CIRCULAR WALKS IN EPPING FOREST
10 circular walks 6 to 18 miles long. Combined they explore the whole forest and its surrounding area. 68 pages. 12 maps. 30 photographs. History notes.
ISBN 1-903627-72-9 @ £8.50

LONG CIRCULAR WALKS IN EASTERN HERTFORDSHIRE
9 walks - 15 to 20 miles long. Beautiful unspoilt walking in rolling countryside full of historical interest. £10.95
ISBN 978-0-9553691-7-9

LONG CIRCULAR WALKS IN WESTERN HERTFORDSHIRE - 9 long walks - 15 to 20 miles.. 112 pages. Wire bound. 55 photographs. 20 detailed maps. £10.95
ISBN 978-0-955651113

SHORT CIRCULAR WALKS AROUND HERTFORD.
3 historical Town walks and four country walks.
ISBN 978-0-9556511-7-5 £9.95

NEW - SHORT CIRCULAR WALKS AROUND BISHOP' STORTFORD

SHORT CIRCULAR WALKS ON THE RIVER STORT NAVIGATION
8 circular walks; 1 End to End walk. Full history and photographic study of this peaceful waterway. 92 pages. 68 photographgs. 12 maps. ISBN 1-903627- 73-7 £11.95

SHORT CIRCULAR WALKS ON THE RIVER LEE NAVIGATION - Southern Volume - Limehouse basin to Hackney Marsh. 5 walks on the Regent Canal, Hertford Union and Limehouse Cut. Including Three Mills and its rivers. The guide also details a 28 mile End to End walk along the Navigation. 68 pages. 10 maps, 30 photographs.
ISBn 1-903627-74-5 £7.95

EPPING FOREST CHALLENGE WALK - 21 MILES. Starts and ends at Waltham Abbey and takes in the whole forest. 44 pages. 6 maps. 10 photos £7.95
ISBN 978-0-9553691-0-0

"St. ALBANS WAY" - 26 mile Pilgrims walk from Waltham Abbey to St. Alban's Cathedral. £7.95
ISBN 978-0-9553691-3-1

NORTH LONDON - THE THREE BOROUGH CHALLENGE WALK - 21 MILES
A walk linking together the three boroughs of Enfield, Barnet and Haringey.
A magnificent countryside walk. Certificate for the successful.
A5. 40 pages. Full colour book.
ISBN 978-0-9556511-9-9 £7.95

NEW - SHORT CIRCULAR WALKS IN EPPING DISTRICT

LONDON PILGRIMAGE WALKS

In medieval times both royalty and layfolk undertook pilgrimages to several holy shrines - to St. Albans, Canterbury and Walsingham via Waltham Abbey. These three books trace the different routes and are walks not just exercise and health but for journeys of the soul and spirituality.

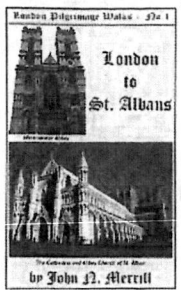

LONDON TO ST. ALBANS - 36 MILES

Starting from Westminster Abbey, the route takes you through North-West London, via more than 30 church's, chapels and places of worship. The basic route is via Regent's Park, Hampstead, Burnt Oak, Stanmore, Elstree and River Ver.
88 pages. 7 maps. 100 photographs. £9.95
ISBN 978-0-9560649-7-4

LONDON TO CANTERBURY - 75 MILES

Starting from Westminster Abbey the route is via Southark Cathedral and River Thames to Greenwich. Then Watling Street to Gravesend, Rochester, Sittingbourne and Faversham to Canterbury. Numerous churchs and historial features are passed.
140 pages. 15 maps. 120 photographs. £12.95
ISBN 978-0-9560649-6-7

LONDON TO WALSINGHAM - 180 MILES

Starting from Holborn or St. Magnus church, the route takes you up the Lee Valley to Waltham Abbey - a pilgrimage centre in its own right. Then onto Ware, Cottered, Royston, Newmarket, Mildenhall, Bury St. Edmunds, Brandon, Swaffham, Fakenham, the Slipper Chapel and Little Walsingham.
256 pages. 41 maps. 243 photographs. £14.95
ISBN 978-0-9564644-2-2

A WALK FOR PEACE - 10 MILES

A Buddhist themed walk from the Tibetan Peace Gardens beside the Imperial War Museum to Battersea Peace Pagoda and onto the Buddhapadipa temple. at Wimbledon.
20 pages. Colour photographs. £3.95

Wherever you are, you are either

on or close to a

John Merrill Walk.

........enjoy!

Illustrated Talks
by Revd. John N. Merrill

*John has countless talks on his recording breaking walks around the world. For a full list contact John - Tel. 01992-762776
Email - marathonhiker@aol.com*

His latest talks -

WALKING TO MONT ST. MICHEL - John has walked here twice - from Farnham via Winchester to Mont St. Michel (200 miles), and from Caen (100 miles) joining the annual pilgrimage walk organised by the Association of Chemins de Mont St. Michel. Both remarkable walks with the final 7km across the exposed sand, mud and rivers to the rock and abbey.

LONDON TO OXFORD PILGRIMAGE WALK - St. Frideswide Way - 93 miles. John discovers and traces the medieval pilgrimage route from Westminster Abbey to Christ Church Cathedral in Oxford, and the shrine of St. Frideswide. Then onto Binsey and her "forgotten" healing well; the Lourdes of the South.

WALKING ESSEX'S COASTLINE - 250 MILES - An exceptional walk around England's second largest county's coastline, rich in history, sea-birds and waders and more than 100 islands. A surprising journey.

WALKING MY WAY - The on going story of John's unique walking life, with some 219,000 miles walked. The stories and tales from his ground breaking walks around the world.

The Art of walking the John Merrill Way.

1. Always set off in the clothes you plan to wear all day, given the weather conditions. Only on sudden changes in the weather will I stop and put on a waterproof or warmer clothing.

2. Set off at a steady comfortable pace, which you can maintain all day. You should end the walk as fresh as when you started.

3. Maintain your pace and don't stop. Stopping for any period of time disrupts your rythmn and takes upwards of a mile (20 mins) to settle back down into the flow/ease of movement.

4. Switch your phone off. Listen and enjoy the countryside - the smell of the flowers, bird song, the rustle of leaves and the tinkling stream, and observe the wildlife.

5. Ignore the mileage and ascents - don't tick the miles or hills, just concentrate on what the walk's goal is. To think otherwise slows you down and makes the walk a struggle rather than a joy. In a similar vein, when ascending just keep a steady pace and keep going. To stop is to disrupt the flow and make the ascent interminable.

6. Whist a walk is a challenge to complete, it is not just exercise. You should enjoy the world around you, the flowers, birds, wildlife and nature and look at and explore the historical buildings and churches that you pass. Industrial complex's have their own beauty. All are part of life's rich tapestry.

7. Remember that for every mile you walk, you extend your life by 21 minutes.

8. A journey of a 1,000 miles begins with a single step and a mile requires 2,000 strides.

"The expert traveller leaves no footprints" Lao Tzu.

THE JOHN MERRILL FOUNDATION LONG DISTANCE WALKING CHARTER FOR THE UK.

1. All path signs to be made of wood and clearly state the right of way designation and destination, with correct mileage/kilometers. Individually designed, logo or symbols is to be encouraged. Variety and individuality is essential.

2. Wooden stiles are preferred to kissing gates. Kissing gates have a fatal flaw - many are not wide enough yo allow a backpacker with his pack to get in and out of without removing the pack. For half the year the central area is wet and muddy. The metal bar stiles with a wide base and narrow neck at thew top should be abolished; they are not suitable for backpackers - all have to take the rucksacks off to get through.
SOS - *Save our stiles* - part of our heritage.

3. All long distance routes to clearly state the start and end of the route on the ground, with an overall map showing the route at each end. Registration boxes at either end for signing in and out.

4. All long distance routes should provide regular places for wild camping. No ammenities required just a place to pitch a tent.

5. All temporary path closures should be notified from the nearest road and not at the start of a particular path - this results in having to walk back. The diversion or temporay alternative route should be clearly well signed.

6. Every walker should be trained to read a map, use a compass and calculate a gride reference. The dependence of modern technology is to be encouraged - but learn the basic skills.

7. All long distance walkers should wear well broken in and good fitting boots, wkith two pairs of socks, and carry the minumum basics in a suitable padded and framed rucksack.

8. All footpaths & rights of way's should be be regularly cleared of brambles, nettles, blow downs, and overhanging branches to allow a walker to pass through comfortably. Paths should be natural earth, not gravel, tarmac or rock slab.

9. Take your rubbish home - pack it in, pack it out.

10. Take only pictures.

11. Admire the flowers but do not pick them.

12. Say "hello" to all walkers that you pass.

13. Leave your headphones, music centre at home so you can enjoy the sounds of nature. Switch your phone off and only use in an emergency.

Pilgrim
Stamp
Pages
- add dates

THE JOHN MERRILL MINISTRY
- a universal monk -
embracing & honouring
all faiths & none.

John has been following his own spiritual path all his life, and is guided. He was brought up as a Christian and confirmed at the age of 13. He then went to a Quaker Boarding School for five years and developed his love for the countryside and walking. He became fascinated with Tibet and whilst retaining his Christian roots, became immersed in Buddhism. For four years he studied at the Tara Buddhist Centre in Derbyshire. He progressed into Daoism and currently attends the Chinese Buddhist Temple (Pure Land Tradition) in London. With his thirst for knowledge and discovery he paid attention to other faiths and appreciated their values. Late in life he decided it was time to reveal his spiritual beliefs and practices and discovered the Interfaith Seminary.

'When the pupil is ready, the teacher will appear'. (Buddhist saying).

Here for two years he learnt in more depth the whole spectrum of faiths , including Jainism, Paganism, Mother Earth, Buddhism, Hinduism, Islam, Judaism, Sikhism, Celtic Worship and Shamanism. This is an ongoing exploration without end. He embraces all faiths, for all have a beauty of their own. All paths/faiths lead to one goal/truth. On July 17th. 2010 he was Ordained as a Multi-faith Minister.

*'May you go in peace, with joy in your heart
and may the divine be always at your side.'*

Using his knowledge and experience he combines many faiths into a simple, caring and devoted services, individually made for each specific occasion, with dignity and honour.
He conducts special Ceremonies -

Popular Funeral Celebrant and member of the Natural Death Society.

* Funerals * Memorial Services * Sermons * Weddings   *Civil Partnerships
* Baby Blessings & Naming
* Rites of Passage * Healing Ceremonies * Pilgimages * Inspirational Talks
Qigong Teacher.   Reiki Prationer.

For further information Contact John on -
Tel/Fax: 01992 - 762776   Mobile. 07910 889429
Email - universalmonk@oulook.com
Ministry site -www.thejohnmerrillministry.co.uk
All Faiths church - www.londoninterfaithchurch.co.uk

Revd. John N. Merrill, HonMUni
32, Holmesdale, Waltham Cross,
Hertfordshire EN8 8QY